STRAIGHT FROM THE HEART

STRAIGHT FROM THE HEART

Thoughts of
JOHN HENRY NEWMAN

Introduced, Chosen and Arranged by
Kevin and Gail Dean

THE THOMAS MORE PRESS
Chicago, Illinois

Copyright © 1990 by Kevin and Gail Greene. All rights reserved. Printed in the United States of America. No part of this publication may be reproduced, stored in a retrieval system, transmitted in any form or by any means, electronic, mechanical, photocopying, recording or otherwise, without the written permission of the publisher, The Thomas More Association, 205 West Monroe Street—Sixth Floor, Chicago, Illinois 60606-5097.

ISBN: 0-88347-250-3

CONTENTS

9. BIOGRAPHICAL INTRODUCTION

THE QUESTION, WHY?

21. Is There a God?
23. But Are You Sure?
25. The Voice Within.
26. Peace Be With You.
27. Real Religion and Theory.
29. Genuine Religion Brings Joy.
30. Adoration.
31. Personal Prayer.
32. The One Thing Necessary.
33. The Face of Christ.
34. Christ's Church in the World.
35. The Life of the Spirit.
36. Religious Experience.
37. The Best Argument for Religion.

CONTEMPORARY ISSUES.

41. All Things For God.
42. Psychology.
44. Boredom.
45. Looking for "Kicks".
47. Drink.
48. Sex.
50. Marriage.
51. Friendship.
52. Success.
53. Suffering.
55. Comforting Others.
56. Conscience First.
57. The Importance of the Individual.
59. My Church . . . Sometimes Wrong.
60. My Country . . . Sometimes Wrong.
61. Every Creed and Class.
62. Progress.
63. A World in Need of Compassion.
65. Social Reform.
66. Education.
68. The First Shall Be Last.

MAN OF MANY INTERESTS.

71. Poetry.
73. Praise to the Holiest.
75. Novels.

76. Music.
78. Architecture.
79. The Art of Teaching.
81. Children.
83. Community.
84. Politics.
86. Sport.
88. Animals.

PERSONAL GLIMPSES.

93. A Young Man's Thoughts.
94. Love the One Thing Needful.
96. Death of a Dear One.
97. This Is My Life.
99. Lead Kindly Light.
101. Peace of Mind.
102. A Failure.
103. More Failure.
105. When Shall We Three Meet Again?
107. Dear Mr. Gladstone.
109. Life's Purpose.
110. The End.

113. SUGGESTED FURTHER READINGS

115. BIBLIOGRAPHY

For our son
Michael Newman Dean

BIOGRAPHICAL INTRODUCTION

IN 1816, a fifteen-year-old boy tried to row around the Isle of Wight in the fog. His mind was probably not filled with the defeat of Napoleon in the previous year, nor with the dropping of income tax, nor with the passing of the Corn Laws, but rather was he preoccupied with a personal crisis.

Born in London in 1801, John Henry Newman was brought up in comfortable circumstances as a member of the Anglican Church. The eldest of six children, he never lacked companions for play, was clever, musical and loved swimming and riding.

While Shelley was running into trouble at Oxford for his atheism and Byron of the many affairs was in the process of separating from his wife, John climbed the cliffs at St. Leonard's with his brother Charles till they could climb no higher and had to be rescued. At seven he began his schooling at a boarding school in Ealing and did exceedingly well.

But at fifteen a double crisis struck his life. He was called home from school to receive the news that his father's bank had failed and the family had to move

STRAIGHT FROM THE HEART

from London to Alton. Mr. Newman never quite recovered.

For John himself there was a personal crisis of another kind. He seems to have been reading the atheistic writings of Paine and Hume and copied out some French verses against the immortality of the soul, to which his reaction was, "How dreadful yet how plausible." Suddenly the whole thing seemed dreadfully implausible. An inner voice which seemed to grow like the approach of distant thunder, filled the boy with awe, sweeping aside the smooth reasoning of Hume as easily as a breeze disperses mist. The experience seems to have been startling in its direct apprehension of an overwhelming Governing Power. John saw himself as "more like a devil than a wicked boy," in the grip of Satanic pride. Truly the beginning of wisdom was the fear of the Lord. Some thirty years before, the young Wordsworth had described a similar experience.

One thing was clear: nothing could reason away a voice which spoke with such authority. Ever after Newman was to insist that the existence of God was as certain as his own existence, "Two only supreme and luminously self-evident beings, myself and my creator." This crisis lasted from August to December. At the time a young evangelical clergyman lent him some books. One treated of the Trinity and the need to search for Truth, "Growth is the only evi-

THOUGHTS OF JOHN HENRY NEWMAN

dence of life." The other introduced him to the early Fathers of the Church.

In 1817 John entered Trinity College, Oxford, where he met John Bowden who was to be a lasting friend. He was welcomed by his tutor, Mr. Short, who was still there in 1878 when Newman returned after an exile of more than thirty years.

Unlike many of the students, John worked hard, practiced his violin and attracted the scorn of some because he would not get drunk. At the end of his first year he won a scholarship of 60 pounds annually for nine years. Keats visited Oxford in the summer of 1817 while composing "Endymion," but seems to have made little impression on John whose mind was turning rapidly from a career in the Law to one in the Church. By 1820 he was ready for his final exams which he almost failed through nerves.

He continued at Oxford studying and coaching students. Among them his brother, Francis, who had the knack of irritating John almost beyond endurance. He never understood John, although the two got on well enough later when they both helped to support their other brother, Charles, who, following a bout of insanity, settled down at Tenby in Wales. Francis, after a tour of the East to spread the Christian message, spent some time teaching at Manchester College where he joined a circle of Unitarians which included the novelist Mrs. Gaskell. She,

STRAIGHT FROM THE HEART

egged on by Dickens, gave vent to her humanitarian feelings by depicting the hell that Manchester workers endured, giving an insider's view which surpassed even the horrors which Friedrich Engels was passing on to his friend, Karl Marx.

John, although devoted to ministering to the poor throughout his life, felt that his particular call was to search for truth and to try and heal society at the root of its trouble. At this time he was writing for an Evangelical paper called "The Christian Observer." His father was disgusted, for John Newman senior considered that his son was becoming more religious than was good for him.

Devoted to his family, John was to help financially when his father went bankrupt in 1821. He was especially fond of his sisters: "O, how I love them," he wrote after giving them communion in 1825. By this time he was a fellow of Oriel College with a university career before him as well as a pastoral ministry.

In 1828, his youngest sister, Mary, died. She was particularly dear to him and her death shocked him into a personal trauma. He later wrote that it brought home to him that he was beginning to prefer intellectual excellence to moral. Throughout his life he never referred to her without tears and kept her anniversary faithfully.

The next youngest sister, Jemima, was also close to John. He confided in her especially when he was tired and disappointed. She never understood his

THOUGHTS OF JOHN HENRY NEWMAN

conversion to Rome and, although they kept in touch, the old intimacy was gone. She felt that the brother she had known was dead.

Harriet, the oldest of the girls, married one of John's students, Tom Mozley. After his conversion John saw little of her.

On his father's death in 1824, John had settled his mother and the girls at Brighton and later they moved to Oxford to be near him. They remained a close family until 1845.

Meanwhile there was work to be done. John threw himself into his tutoring and preaching, making many friends and some enemies as well. Robert Peel, the Member of Parliament for Oxford, was at the beginning of a distinguished career during which he founded the police force and the conservative party, but he was too inclined to interfere in Church matters for Newman, who felt that a parliament which included non-believers among its members had little right to meddle in ecclesiastical affairs. At election time he campaigned against Peel and helped to unseat him. This did Peel little harm, for he immediately found a safe borough (reform of parliament was still in the future). Newman, however, suffered financially, for this was one of the reasons that caused the university authorities to starve him of pupils, which meant a loss of 600 pounds per year.

When the father of a sick friend, Hurrell Froude, proposed a trip abroad, John was persuaded to go. In

STRAIGHT FROM THE HEART

Rome, he decided to stay on alone when his companions returned to England. He wished to wander by himself and see the ordinary people of Italy. While in Sicily he fell ill and almost died of a fever, at the same time experiencing an inner crisis that centered around a feeling of his own utter uselessness. This journey into darkness produced his poem "Lead, Kindly Light" and left him with the clear conviction that he "had a work to do in England."

On returning to Oxford, his friend John Keble preached a sermon on "National Apostasy." It started a furore in Oxford that spread through the nation during the next few years. It was 1833; Newman and his friends were discovering the ancient writings of the Church and were convinced that many Christians, even some in high places, were going along with the spirit of the age, a spirit of disbelief. For such, the teachings of Christ, handed down from the first days of the Church, needed updating, adapting, changing to suit the new era of scientific progress. For Newman and his friends such thinking was a betrayal of what the Church stood for; they hurled themselves into the battle with zest. In 1836, John's mother died and at about the same time his sisters married, leaving him free to devote himself to preaching, writing, studying; his influence grew. People flocked to hear him. At the same time, he continued his normal pastoral work of baptisms, weddings, funerals, visiting the sick, preparing for con-

THOUGHTS OF JOHN HENRY NEWMAN

firmation. By 1837, as the young Queen Victoria ascended the throne, Newman was a national figure.

A cloud passed over him in 1839 when his studies led him to suspect that his beloved Church might be in error and Rome, for all her corruptions, might be right. He wrote a tract trying to reconcile the articles of the Church of England with Catholic beliefs. A storm of powerful and, at times, frenzied opposition broke over him. He retired to the peace of Littlemore, just outside Oxford, to pray and study. Others came to join him there. In 1843 he felt he had to resign his ministry and set himself to work out God's will by prayer and writing his thoughts on the development of Christian teaching. Whilst engaged in this task, he asked an Italian priest, Dominic Barberi, to receive him into the Roman Church. In 1847, with his friend Ambrose St. John, he was ordained a priest in Rome. There he discovered the rule of life of St. Philip Neri, which he was to adapt for a community in England.

And so, as Europe was being convulsed by revolution, as famine visited Ireland, driving thousands of her children to join the poor of England's cities, Newman started his community in Birmingham, hoping to play some small part in the second Spring of the Church's life, which he felt was beginning. The Oratory, as it was called, began in an old gin distillery. The Community served the local Catholics with the Sacraments and the teaching of the Church. There were special talks for children but, at first, no school, for, from the age of seven, youngsters worked from morning till night. Factory girls formed a choir with Newman at the organ. Birmingham was smelly, the confessionals bugridden and the cholera came to visit; but Newman loved his new life. A second Oratory was established in London.

These years brought their trials and disappointments too, however. In a lecture in 1851, Newman attacked an ex-Catholic priest, Giacomo Achilli. The man had been defrocked for seducing young girls and had discovered that there was a market for scurrilous tales against his former brethren. He took Newman to court for libel and won his case, in spite of his known character and the presence in court of witnesses from Italy, including one of his victims. Newman was fined and given a stiff lecture. Then there was the call to found a university in Ireland. He went, only to find that most of the Bishops did not want it. Archbishop Cullen, who did, wanted an establishment under his control—not quite Newman's idea of a university. Nevertheless he gathered together a distinguished staff and the university began its life. Newman crossed and recrossed the Irish Sea over fifty times in the cause of education. There were problems with his Oratory at home at this time: there was a split with the London Oratory which went its own way under Fr. Faber. Newman resigned from the university in 1857; it never developed as he had hoped.

THOUGHTS OF JOHN HENRY NEWMAN

There were other problems: a plan to translate the Bible came to nothing; his first attempt to found a school failed (though it was to succeed later), an article of his, "On Consulting the Laity in Matters of Doctrine," was misunderstood at Rome, leaving him under a cloud of suspicion for years. Newman discovered that, if he had felt the Anglican Church to be lacking in authority, Rome could be heavy-handed indeed; if the English Church had needed to hold to tradition, Rome needed to march a little. It would be going too far to say he ever regretted his change, but it has taken over a century for many of his ideas to be officially accepted in the Church of Rome.

In 1863, Newman received a magazine in which Charles Kingsley had written the astonishing remark that Roman Catholic clergy are urged to fight the evil of the world not with truth but with cunning, a doctrine which he attributed to Newman.

It is said that Newman stood at his desk in his library for hours at a time until he had produced his best-known work, *Apologia Pro Vita Sua*. An account of his own search for truth, it was a best-seller and left no doubt in anyone's mind as to where its author stood in the matter of reverence for truth. It restored Newman to a position of influence again. Other works followed; his poem "The Deam of Gerontius" was very popular; The *Grammar of Assent* was a more learned work. There were other articles and essays which did not please everybody. Newman did

STRAIGHT FROM THE HEART

not mind; "In essentials unity, in other things freedom" was his motto. In the 1870s, after the definition of papal infallibility, it fell to him to point out to no less than Mr. Gladstone that English Catholics were no less loyal to Queen Victoria than her other subjects. Old friends died, younger men came to join him at the Oratory. Oxford gave him an honorary fellowship; Pope Leo XIII made him a Cardinal of the Church (he took as his motto, "Heart speaks to Heart"). Even the Lord Chief Justice (whose father had once lectured Newman at the Achilli trial) confessed to being awestruck in the old priest's presence. To the boys of his school, though, he was "Old Jack" and remained so till the end.

He died quietly on the 11th of August, 1890, and was buried next to his friend, Ambrose St. John, at Rednal in Birmingham.

THE QUESTION, WHY?

Our age has devoted itself with spectacular results to answering the question, How do things work? We know how to split the atom, how to travel to the moon, how to make people live longer. Newman calls us to reflect on the fundamental question, Why?

THOUGHTS OF JOHN HENRY NEWMAN

IS THERE A GOD?

Newman answered this question by referring to his own experience of the voice of conscience. He was quite well aware of the arguments put forward to prove God's existence but while "I have no intention whatever of denying the beauty and the cogency of the arguments . . . I question much, whether in matter of fact, they make and keep men Christians."

This is conscience; and, from the nature of the case, its very existence carries on our minds to a Being exterior to ourselves; for else whence did it come? and to a Being superior to ourselves; else whence its strange troublesome peremptoriness? I say, without going on to the question *what* it says, and whether its particular dictates are always as clear and consistent as they might be, its very existence throws us out of ourselves, and beyond ourselves, to go and seek for Him in the height and depth, whose Voice it is. As the sunshine implies that the sun is in the heavens, though we may not see it, as a knocking at our doors at night implies the presence of one outside in the dark who asks for admittance, so this Word within us, not only instructs us up to a certain point, but necessarily raises our minds to the idea of a Teacher, an unseen teacher: and in proportion as we listen to that Word and use it, not only do we learn more from it, not only do its

STRAIGHT FROM THE HEART

dictates become clearer and its lessons broader and its principles more consistent, but its very tone is louder and more authoritative and constraining.

Sermons Preached on Various Occasions

THOUGHTS OF JOHN HENRY NEWMAN

BUT ARE YOU SURE?

In an age that looked for scientific proof and logical conclusions about everything, Newman pointed out that sane people enjoy certainty about many things without such proofs, indeed would not dream of demanding them in such matters as the fact that Great Britain is an island or that we shall die or that the Latin classics were not written in the thirteenth century. The mind has its own ways of reaching certainty apart from mere logic or science. For himself, he confessed that "the being of a God is, to my own apprehension, encompassed with most difficulty, yet borne in upon our minds with most power." In his "Apologia" he expressed his certainty of God as follows:

If I am asked why I believe in a God, I answer that it is because I believe in myself, for I feel it impossible to believe in my own existence (and of that I am quite sure) without believing also in the existence of Him, who lives as a personal, All-seeing, All-judging, Being in my conscience."

In later life he expressed the same thought with equal clarity and certainty in the "Meditations and Devotions":

Almighty God, Thou art the One Infinite Fulness . . . I hold this as a matter of reason, though my imagina-

STRAIGHT FROM THE HEART

tion starts from it . . . I hold it from that long and intimate familiarity with it, so that it is part of my rational nature to hold it; because I am so constituted and made up upon the idea of it, as a keystone, that not to hold it would be to break my mind to pieces. I hold it from that intimate perception of it in my conscience, as a fact present to me, that I feel it as easy to deny my own personality as the personality of God, and have lost my grounds for believing that I exist myself, if I deny existence to Him.

Apologia
Meditations and Devotions

THOUGHTS OF JOHN HENRY NEWMAN

THE VOICE WITHIN.

For Newman the most fundamental and important experience of being human was the awareness of the voice of conscience. Obedience here is what gives a human life wholeness and direction. All through his life Newman insisted on this. Perhaps he may be called the great preacher of the doctrine of conscience.

Whether a man be born in pagan darkness, or in some corruption of revealed religion,—whether he has heard the Name of the Saviour of the world or not,—whether he be the slave of some superstition,—or is in possession of some portions of Scripture, and treats the inspired word as a sort of philosophical book, which he interprets for himself, and comes to certain conclusions about its teaching,—in any case, he has within his breast a certain commanding dictate, not a mere sentiment, not a mere opinion or impression, or view of things, but a law, an authoritative voice, bidding him do certain things and avoid others.

Sermons Preached On Various Occasions

STRAIGHT FROM THE HEART

PEACE BE WITH YOU.

Few teachers have insisted upon purity of conscience as Newman did. He has even been accused of basing his preaching upon fear. But his insistence upon this is balanced by his realistic awareness, not only of human frailty but also of the limits of the human mind. God's will must be sought in all things, but in practical affairs probability is the guide to life and we must be content with the kind of certitude that is possible in moral matters.

We must take the constitution of the human mind as we find it, and not as we may judge it ought to be . . . introspection of our intellectual operations is not the best means of preserving us from intellectual hesitations. To meddle with the springs of thought and action is really to weaken them . . . I observe that moral evidence and moral certitude are all that we can attain, not only in the case of ethical and spiritual subjects, such as religion, but of terrestrial and cosmical questions also . . . My first elementary lesson of duty is that of resignation to the laws of my nature, whatever they are; my first disobedience is to be impatient at what I am, and to indulge an ambitious aspiration after what I cannot be, to cherish a distrust of my powers, and to desire to change laws which are identical with myself.

Grammar of Assent

THOUGHTS OF JOHN HENRY NEWMAN

REAL RELIGION AND THEORY.

Newman could mix it with the cleverest of thinkers when he chose. In the matter of religion, however, he sided very firmly with the ordinary believer who often finds it very difficult to put into words reasons for believing and even more difficult to argue against those who attack religion. Newman believed that sincere and well-founded belief was based primarily on a good conscience rather than upon a trained intellect. In fact he points out clearly and eloquently that intellectuals frequently use their gifts unwisely and wrongly, landing themselves further and further from the truth. In 1831 he made this point clearly in a sermon preached before the university at Oxford.

There is no act on God's part, no truth of religion, to which a captious Reason may not find objections; and in truth the evidence and matter of Revelation are not addressed to the mere unstable Reason of man, nor can hope for any certain or adequate reception with it. Divine Wisdom speaks, not to the world, but to her own children, or those who have been already under her teaching, and who, knowing her voice, understand her words, and are suitable judges of them. These justify her.... So alert is the instinctive power of an educated conscience, that by some secret faculty, and without any intelligible reasoning process, it seems to detect moral truth wherever it

STRAIGHT FROM THE HEART

lies hid, and feels a conviction of its own accuracy which bystanders cannot account for; and this especially in the case of Revealed Religion.

University Sermons

THOUGHTS OF JOHN HENRY NEWMAN

GENUINE RELIGION BRINGS JOY.

Newman often described the sadness of what he called natural religion. The ancient pagan world was marked by "the tears of things." Natural religion springs from conscience and conscience brings fear. This basic human experience is precious and to be cherished but it is only an anticipation of the revelation of God which drives out fear by offering forgiveness and grace.

A little religion makes us afraid; when a little light is poured in upon the conscience, there is a darkness visible; nothing but sights of woe and terror; the glory of God alarms while it shines around. His holiness, the range and difficulties of His commandments, the greatness of His power, the faithfulness of His word, frighten the sinner, and men, seeing him afraid, think religion has made him so, whereas he is not yet religious at all . . . he is merely conscience-stricken. But religion itself, far from inculcating alarm and terror, says, in the words of the angel, "Fear not."

Parochial and Plain Sermons, VIII 17

STRAIGHT FROM THE HEART
ADORATION.

If, as some psychologists believe, we of the twentieth century have lost the sense of the numinous, the feeling of awe before the Almighty, it was certainly not lacking in Newman's make-up. He felt it in the great cathedrals of England (in old age, scruffy and unrecognized, he was thrown out of St. Paul's entrance where he was listening to Evensong) and he found it in the churches of Rome and of England. An instance of this last may be found in the novel "Loss and Gain."

The church-door came first, and, as it was open, he entered it. It apparently was filling for service ... A profusion of candles were lighting at the High Altar, which stood in the centre of a semi-circular apse. There were side-altars—perhaps half a dozen; most of them without lights, but, even here, solitary worshippers might be seen. Over one was a large old Crucifix with a lamp, and this had a succession of visitors. ... At length the church got very full; rich and poor were mixed together ... A set of boys and children, mixed with some old crones, had got possession of the altar rail, and were hugging it with restless motions, as if in expectation.

Loss and Gain

THOUGHTS OF JOHN HENRY NEWMAN

PERSONAL PRAYER.

Praying for Newman was much more than saying prayers according to set formulas, important though these might be. Prayer for him is a habit of mind, as he describes so beautifully in a sermon of 1829.

... As our bodily life discovers itself by its activity, so is the presence of the Holy Spirit in us discovered by a spiritual activity; and this activity is the spirit of continual prayer ... for the new birth of the Holy Spirit sets the soul in motion in a heavenly way; it gives us good thoughts and desires, enlightens and purifies us, and prompts us to seek God ... Thus the true Christian pierces through the veil of this world and sees the next. He holds intercourse with it; he addresses God as a child might address his parent, with as clear a view of Him, and with as unmixed a confidence in Him.

Parochial and Plain Sermons, VII 15

STRAIGHT FROM THE HEART

THE ONE THING NECESSARY.

For Newman the deepest need of the human spirit at all times and in all places was to find and feed on the life of the Spirit and the image of Christ. Here is the bond of nations, here the great remedy for the divisions of the human race.

His preachers have imprinted the Image or idea of Himself in the minds of His subjects individually; and that Image, apprehended and worshipped in individual minds, becomes a principle of association and a real bond of those subjects one with another, who are thus united to the body by being united to that Image; and moreover that Image, which is their moral life, when they have been already converted, is also the original instrument of their conversion. It is the Image of Him who fulfills the one great need of human nature, the Healer of its wounds, the Physician of the soul, this Image it is which both creates faith, and then rewards it.

Grammar of Assent

THOUGHTS OF JOHN HENRY NEWMAN

THE FACE OF CHRIST.

The world, Newman believed, was in need of God, not so much theories and ideas about God, but God Himself in the hearts and minds of individuals. Theories touch only the mind, people reach the heart and a real meeting with the Christ of the Gospels was the most fundamental way of healing the ills of the world. Throughout his life Newman kept his gaze on the world's saviour even to his last years from which this meditation comes.

I see the figure of a man, whether young or old I cannot tell. He may be fifty or He may be thirty. Sometimes he looks one, sometimes the other. There is something inexpressible about His face which I cannot solve. Perhaps, as he bears all burdens, he bears that of old age too. But so it is; His face is at once most venerable, yet most childlike, most calm, most sweet, most modest, beaming with sanctity and with loving-kindness. His eyes rivet me and move my heart. His breath is all fragrant, and transports me out of myself. Oh, I will look upon that face for ever, and will not cease.

Meditations and Devotions

STRAIGHT FROM THE HEART

CHRIST'S CHURCH IN THE WORLD.

Statistics today reveal what the pages of history have always shown, that pride and greed rule, that pleasure-seeking fills lives that in two thousand years "the Gospel has not materially changed more than the surface of things." Is the Church then irrelevant, as her numerical decline seems to indicate in many Western countries?

Christ came . . . not to convert the world, but "to purify unto himself a peculiar people, zealous of good works;" not to sanctify this evil world but to "deliver us out of this present evil world . . . not to turn the whole earth into a heaven, but to bring down a heaven upon earth. This has been the real triumph of the Gospel, to raise those beyond themselves and beyond human nature, in whatever rank and condition of life, whose wills mysteriously co-operate with God's grace, who, while God visits them, really fear and really obey God, whatever be the unknown reason why one man obeys Him and another not. It has made men saints, and brought into existence specimens of faith and holiness, which without it are unknown and impossible.

Parochial and Plain Sermons, IV 10

THOUGHTS OF JOHN HENRY NEWMAN

THE LIFE OF THE SPIRIT.

For Newman prayer was a continual exercise. It was the language of heaven. He believed strongly in the effectiveness of asking for things and even warned against asking for favours which could turn out to be more than the asker had bargained for.

. . . It is true that religious men have their prayers answered in a wonderful way, and with sufficient distinctness to be, in addition to other evidences, a ground of confidence to them that God is with them . . . There are prayers which we have no confidence will be answered; but there are others which, as the experience of all ages assures us, are dangerous ones, because they are so effectual. Often the word has passed the tongue, and is written in heaven, and in spite of our own change of wish it is accomplished. Among such prayers are prayers for affliction.

Sermons on Subjects of the Day

STRAIGHT FROM THE HEART

RELIGIOUS EXPERIENCE.

For Newman religion was always a matter of the whole person, heart and mind. At times he seems to have had an unusually vivid awareness of the presence of God, as this sermon from 1841 indicates.

". . . If you can recollect times when you visited holy places, and certainly gained there a manifestation such as the world could not give; or if sermons have come to you with power, and have been blessed to our spiritual good, or if your soul has been, as it were, transfigured within you, when you came to the Most Holy Sacrament . . . or if at ordinations you have been partakers of an indescribable influence, and almost savour of grace, though you realised it not at the time; or if strange providences and almost supernatural coincidences have hung about the Church's ordinances; if mercies or judgments have descended through them upon yourselves, or upon those about you; or if you have experience of deathbeds and know how full of hope the children of our church can die;—O pause ere you doubt that we have a divine presence among us still, and have not to seek it."

Sermons on Subjects of the Day

THOUGHTS OF JOHN HENRY NEWMAN

THE BEST ARGUMENT FOR RELIGION.

Newman did not deny the usefulness of constructing arguments to meet the difficulties which are raised against religion, nor was he against the arguments for God's presence in the visible world which theologians provide. But for many he considered there was a better way.

... The best argument, better than all the books in the world, better than all that astronomy, and geology, and physiology, and all the other sciences, can supply,—an argument intelligible to those who cannot read as well as to those who can,—an argument which is "within us,"—an argument intellectually conclusive, and practically persuasive, whether for proving the Being of God, or for laying the ground for Christianity,—is that which arises out of a careful attention to the teachings of our heart, and a comparison between the claims of conscience and the announcements of the Gospel.

Sermons Preached on Various Occasions

CONTEMPORARY ISSUES.

Considered by many to be one of the finest minds of his day, Newman often had occasion to turn his attention to the problems which face everybody and says many things which are illuminating and relevant to our time.

THOUGHTS OF JOHN HENRY NEWMAN

ALL THINGS FOR GOD.

When Newman was in Rome he became especially attracted to the founder of the Oratory, St. Philip Neri. One of the qualities he most admired in this sixteenth-century Italian was the manner in which he set out in the demoralized Rome of his day, to help people sanctify the ordinary things in life.

St. Philip Neri bears the title of the Apostle of Rome. Why? Was he a great divine? no; he never professed any theological learning, sufficiently as he was versed in it . . . Did he undertake to form great saints? not so . . . he turned himself . . . to the sanctification of ordinary men . . . He lived in an age, too, when literature and art were receiving their fullest development, and commencing their benign reign over the populations of Europe, and his work was not to destroy or supersede these good gifts of God, but . . . to sanctify poetry, and history, and painting and music, to the glory of the Giver.

Sermons Preached on Various Occasions

STRAIGHT FROM THE HEART
PSYCHOLOGY.

Some three quarters of a century before Freud began to publish his theories Newman was analyzing the human psyche, probing the depths of its guilt and suggesting his own ways to wholeness in the sermons he preached as a clergyman at Oxford.

Day and night follow each other not more surely than punishment comes upon sin. Whether the sin be great or little, momentary or habitual, wilful or through infirmity, its own peculiar punishment seems, according to the law of nature, to follow, as far as our experience of that law carries us ... and first of all it is natural to reflect on the probable influence on us of sins committed in our childhood, and even infancy which we never realised or have altogether forgotten ... childrens' minds are impressible in a very singular way ... there is no extravagance in the idea that passing sins then contracted and forgotten forever afterwards, should so affect the soul as to cause those moral differences between man and man which ... are too clear to be denied ... if a man is taken at unawares, an apparently small sin leads to consequences in years and ages to come so fearful, that one can hardly dare to contemplate them ...

Single sins indulged or neglected are often the cause of other defects of character, which seem to have no connection with them ...

THOUGHTS OF JOHN HENRY NEWMAN

Suppose, for instance, that a man is naturally resentful and unforgiving. He may, in spite of this, have a great number of excellences . . . great faith, great sanctity . . . he thinks himself devoted to God . . . and so he is . . . but, in spite of all this, he has just one fault in a different direction,—there is a fault out of sight. He forgets that in spite of this harmony between all within and all without for twenty three hours of the day, there is one subject, just now and then recurring, which jars with his mind—there is just one string out of tune . . . Who can pretend to estimate the effect of this apparently slight transgression upon the spiritual state of any one of us? . . . What is the real condition of our heart itself?

Parochial and Plain Sermons, IV 3

STRAIGHT FROM THE HEART

BOREDOM.

"The Shining arrow that was Newman"; this phrase was used by G. K. Chesterton to describe one who never knew the deep-seated boredom that is part of the lives of so many people today. Even the young complain, "I'm bored." Newman believed that from the moment of his conception right into the heart of eternity there was a purpose in his existence. He sought it always.

God has created all things for good; all things for their greatest good; everything for its own good. What is the good of one is not the good of another; what makes one man happy would make another unhappy. God has determined, unless I interfere with His plan, that I should reach that which will be my greatest happiness. He looks on me individually, He calls me by name, He knows what I can do, what I can best be, what is my greatest happiness, and he means to give it to me.

Meditations and Devotions

THOUGHTS OF JOHN HENRY NEWMAN

LOOKING FOR "KICKS."

Drugs, sexual promiscuity and drunkenness were not unknown in the nineteenth century, though horror and pornographic videos had not yet been produced by the new technology. Newman's own recreations were just that: a re-making of life's energies. He was a wide reader, loved walking, rode a lot in his earlier years, enjoyed making music, wrote poetry, had endless discussions with friends, visited zoos, enjoyed nature. But in his life and writing there is a sense of purpose, a freedom from boredom and a care to keep the example of Christ always in his mind which makes seeking for "kicks" seem a puerile objective, beneath the contempt of a Christian who is, be definition, called each day to take up the cross which is the way to life.

And lastly, O my dear Lord, though I am so very weak that I am not fit to ask thee for suffering as a gift, and have not strength to do so, at least I will beg of thee grace to meet suffering well, when Thou in Thy love and wisdom dost bring it upon me. Let me bear pain, reproach, disappointment, slander, anxiety, suspense as Thou wouldst have me . . . I wish to bear insult meekly, and to return good for evil. I wish to humble myself in all things, and to be silent when I am ill-used, and to be patient when sorrow or pain is

STRAIGHT FROM THE HEART

prolonged, and all for the love of Thee and Thy cross, knowing that in this way I shall gain the promise both of this life and of the next.

Meditations and Devotions

THOUGHTS OF JOHN HENRY NEWMAN

DRINK.

Newman was not against drink. When he went to Oxford as a student he found that many of the young men regarded getting drunk as a perfectly acceptable pastime, just as many people do today. He would drink wine with them but would not get drunk, even when his fellow students tried to intimidate him. He put his views on drink clearly and simply in a sermon of 1843.

God has given us "wine that maketh glad the heart of man, and oil to make him a cheerful countenance, and bread to strengthen man's heart." And these good gifts of his, by which our life is strengthened, send the soul forth out of itself in search of sympathy and fellowship; they end not in themselves, nor can be enjoyed in solitude; they create and convey, and blend with social feelings; they are means and tokens of mutual goodwill and kindness; or, to speak more religiously, they are of a sacramental nature. They are intended by being partaken in common, to open our hearts towards each other in love; and this being the case, we may judge how fearful is the abuse of God's gifts in riot or sensuality, for it is in some sort a profanation of a Divine ordinance, a sacrilege.

Sermons on Subjects of the Day

STRAIGHT FROM THE HEART

SEX.

For Newman it was clear that sex was exclusively part of marriage, as far as a Christian was concerned. As a student of history and the classics he was well aware of the perversions and selfish uses of sex that are available and even to be expected among pagans. He thought that to meet such things in the classics could be something of a preparation for adult life, in the sense that one might be prepared and fore-armed against them. Marriage he regarded, from the partners' point of view, as a school of growth in love and, for most, a virtually necessary condition for the disciplining of the instinct of selfishness.

Men who have no tie on them, who have no calls on their daily sympathy and tenderness, who have no one's comfort to consult, who can move about as they please, and indulge the love of variety and the restless humours which are so congenial to the minds of most men, are very unfavourably situated for obtaining that heavenly gift, which is . . . "the very bond of peace and of all virtues." On the other hand I cannot fancy any state of life more favourable for the exercise of high Christian principle, and the matured and refined Christian spirit . . . than that of persons who differ in tastes and general character, being obliged by circumstances to live together, and mutually to accommodate to each other their respec-

THOUGHTS OF JOHN HENRY NEWMAN

tive wishes and pursuits.—And this is one among the many providential benefits ... arising out of the Holy Estate of Matrimony; which not only calls out the tenderest and gentlest feelings of our nature, but, where persons do their duty, must be in various ways more or less a state of self-denial.

Parochial and Plain Sermons, II 5

STRAIGHT FROM THE HEART

MARRIAGE.

Newman never married. From early in life he had the conviction that marriage was not for him, although, as a young man he wavered a couple of times in his resolution. No one knows who might have been the occasion of his second thoughts. Certainly in his first curacy at Oxford the parishioners had him and the vicar's daughter married off. Then when his sister Mary died there entered the family circle Maria Giberne, whose friendship lasted until she died in a convent in 1885. Although he finally decided that his mission in life was too demanding to allow him to marry, he was not unaware of the blessings of the married state as his poem, "The Married and the Single," shows.

> Nay, list again! Who seek its kindly chain
> A second self, a double presence gain;
> Hands, eyes and ears, to act or suffer here,
> Till e'en the weak inspire both love and fear,—
> A comrade's sigh to sooth when cares annoy,
> A comrade's smile to elevate his joy . . .
> But wife and offspring, goods which go or stay,
> Teach us our need and make us trust and pray.
> Take love away and life would be defaced,
> A ghastly vision on a howling waste . . .
>
>   Verses on Various Occasions

THOUGHTS OF JOHN HENRY NEWMAN

FRIENDSHIP.

Though Newman spoke often of the need of commune with God alone, he was no solitary. All his life he needed and was surrounded by friends. First his family, then, as a student, when he enjoyed the special friendship of John Bowden. Later he had other special friends. When the great break came in his life in 1845 and he left his work and those he loved, new friends came to him, both men and women; his last great friendship was with Ambrose St. John, a companion for some thirty years who died in 1875. Newman wept and said, "I do not expect ever to get over the loss I have had." He was a great believer in love of relations and friends, as he explained in a sermon of that title in 1831.

By trying to love our relations and friends, by submitting to their wishes, though contrary to our own, by bearing with their infirmities, by overcoming their occasional waywardness by kindness, by dwelling on their excellences, and trying to copy them, thus it is that we form in our hearts that root of charity, which, though small at first, may, like the mustard seed, at last even overshadow the earth ... Vain talkers about philanthropy ... usually show the emptiness of their profession, by being morose and cruel in the private relations of life, which they seem to count as subjects beneath their notice.

Parochial and Plain Sermons, II 2

STRAIGHT FROM THE HEART

SUCCESS.

Ambition to succeed in the world was not one of Newman's traits. He wrote in a letter of 1830, "One thing I have earnestly desired for years, and I trust in sincerity—that I may never be rich; and I will add (though here I am more sincere at some times than at others) that I may never rise in the Church." To our age which worships success and self-promotion he may seem irrelevant, but the unambitious, simple, straightforward person has something to contribute to society, as he pointed out in a sermon on Nathaniel, the man without guile, which dates from 1831.

This character of mind is something far above the generality of men . . . and the instances which we may every now and then discover of it among Christians will be an evidence to us, if evidence be wanting, that, in spite of all that grovelling minds may say about the necessity of acquaintance with the world and with sin, in order to get on well in life, yet, after all, inexperienced guilelessness carries a man on as safely and more happily . . . (such men) take everything in good part which happens to them, and make the best of everyone; thus they have always something to be pleased with, not seeing the bad, and keenly sensible of the good. And communicating their own happy peace to those around them, they really diminish the evils of life in society at large . . .
Parochial and Plain Sermons, II 27

THOUGHTS OF JOHN HENRY NEWMAN

SUFFERING.

Newman had his fair share of life's sufferings; death of dear ones, illness, anxiety, loss of friends, all of which he bore patiently. He was well aware of the need to take up daily the cross that comes from God. He was not one of those, however, who sought suffering. His balanced approach to Christian acceptance of the cross was based on an awareness of his own weakness and a great care to find the will of God rather than the will of Newman. In the first passage, preached in 1835, he shows a very realistic awareness of what suffering can do to people. The second is a prayer of deep faith in God's power to use suffering for His own good purposes. It was written towards the end of Newman's life.

I would go so far as to say, not only that pain does not commonly improve us, but that without care it has a strong tendency to do our souls harm, viz., by making us selfish; an effect produced even when it does us good in other ways. Weak health, for instance, instead of opening the heart, often makes a man supremely careful of his bodily ease and well-being. Men find an excuse in their infirmities for some extraordinary attention to their comforts . . . They become querulous, self-willed, fastidious, and egotistical.

Whatever, wherever I am, I can never be thrown away. If I am in sickness, my sickness may serve

STRAIGHT FROM THE HEART

Him; in perplexity, my perplexity may serve Him; if I am in sorrow, my sorrow may serve Him. My sickness or perplexity or sorrow may be necessary causes of some great end, which is quite beyond us. He does nothing in vain; He may prolong my life, He may shorten it; He knows what He is about. He may take away my friends, he may throw me among strangers, He may make me feel desolate, make my spirits sink, hide the future from me—still He knows what He is about.

Parochial and Plain Sermons, III 11
Meditations and Devotions

THOUGHTS OF JOHN HENRY NEWMAN
COMFORTING OTHERS.

By 1834 Newman had lost his sister Mary. "Dear Mary seems embodied in every tree and hid behind every hill," he wrote, and passed through a great personal crisis in consequence. It was brought home to him that he had betrayed his calling by preferring intellectual to moral excellence. In 1833 he almost died while in Sicily and had a strange experience that he was called to do some work in England. He was frequently called upon to counsel others and in 1834 pointed out that comforting others is a gift that comes from having passed through trial and having needed comfort oneself.

Man is born to trouble "as the sparks fly upward." More or less, we all have our severe trials of pain and sorrow. If we go on for some years in the world's sunshine, it is only that troubles, when they come, should fall heavier. Such at least is the general rule. Sooner or later we fare as other men; happier than they only if we learn to bear our portion more religiously; and more favoured if we fall in with those who themselves have suffered, and can aid us with their sympathy and their experience. And then, while we profit from what they can give us, we may learn from them freely to give what we have freely received, comforting in turn others with the comfort which our brethren have given us from God.

Parochial and Plain Sermons, V 21

STRAIGHT FROM THE HEART
CONSCIENCE FIRST.

In matters of religious belief Newman proclaimed the primacy of the individual conscience. If he found the Anglican Church of his early years to be wanting in authority, the Roman Church contained individuals who took upon themselves to use authority with little sense of the presence of the Spirit in lay Christians. Newman was an old man who had suffered much in silence from such people when in 1870 he produced his "Grammar of Assent," a book that had long been in the making in his mind.

In religious enquiry each of us can speak only for himself, and for himself he has a right to speak. His own experiences are enough for himself, but he cannot speak for others: he cannot lay down the law; he can only bring his own experiences to the common stock of psychological facts. He knows what has satisfied and satisfies himself . . . his own business is to speak for himself. He uses the words of the Samaritans to their countrywoman, when our Lord had remained with them for two days, "Now we believe, not for thy saying, for we have heard Him ourselves and know that this is indeed the saviour of the world."

Grammar of Assent

THOUGHTS OF JOHN HENRY NEWMAN

THE IMPORTANCE OF THE INDIVIDUAL.

Newman found in the Roman Catholic Church a tendency to centralize. Decisions were taken at Rome. The danger of this, he saw, was to take away individual responsibility. Rome could not see everything, did not know all the circumstances. In England in the 1860s Catholics were officially forbidden to attend Protestant universities. When the future poet, Gerard Manley Hopkins, still at university, became a Catholic, Newman, who received him, advised him to finish his course and get the best degree he could. Newman had indicated the importance of ordinary Christians who also had the gift of the Spirit, in an article about the early Church in 1859. He reprinted and explained it in 1871.

... Taking a wide view of the history (of the fourth century), we are obliged to say that the governing body of the Church came short, and the governed were pre-eminent in faith, zeal, courage, and constancy ... A Pope as a private doctor, and much more, bishops, when not teaching formally, may err, as we find they did err, in the fourth century ... the body of the episcopate was unfaithful to its commission, while the body of the laity was faithful to its baptism ... at one time the pope ... at other times ... councils (of bishops), said what they should not have

STRAIGHT FROM THE HEART

said, or did what obscured and compromised revealed truth.

The Arians of the Fourth Century

THOUGHTS OF JOHN HENRY NEWMAN

MY CHURCH ... SOMETIMES WRONG.

Newman held that the Church of Christ, in its essential teaching, exhibits all the qualities of a divine teacher, never contradicting herself and showing a development of ideas that calls forth "admiration, reverence, love and gratitude." Nevertheless, though having divine gifts, the Church is made up of human beings. Hence in a sermon of 1850 he felt it useful to point out that the Church's leaders are as human as everybody else.

Why need it surprise, if in barbarous ages, or in ages of luxury, there have been bishops, or abbots, or priests who have forgotten themselves and their God, and served the world or the flesh, and have perished in that evil service? What triumph is it, though in a long line of between two and three hundred popes, amid martyrs, confessors, doctors, sage rulers, and loving fathers of their people, one or two or three are found who fulfill the Lord's description of the wicked servant...? What will come of it, though we grant that at this time or that, here or there, mistakes in policy, or ill-advised measures, or timidity, or vacillation in action, or secular maxims, or inhumanity, or narrowness of mind, have seemed to influence the Church's action or her bearing towards her children? I can only say that, taking man as he is, it would be a miracle were such offenses altogether absent from her history.

Sermons Preached on Various Occasions

STRAIGHT FROM THE HEART

MY COUNTRY . . . SOMETIMES WRONG.

Although Newman was very much an Englishman (he noted carefully the occasion when he saw Queen Victoria in 1834 and defended the right of English Catholics not to feel obliged to use devotions that might be suitable for Italians) he was well aware of the wrongs for which England was responsible throughout the world, as he illustrates in this extract from his "Historical Sketches."

(The Englishman) comes among the Irish people as the representative of persons, and actions, and catastrophes, which it is not pleasant to anyone to think about; that he is responsible for the deeds of his forefathers, and of his contemporary Parliaments and Executive; that he is one of a strong, unscrupulous, tyrannous race, standing upon the soil of the injured. He does not bear in mind that it is as easy to forget injuring, as it is difficult to forget being injured. He does not admit, even in his imagination, the judgement and the sentence which the past history of Erin sternly pronounces upon him.

Historical Sketches

THOUGHTS OF JOHN HENRY NEWMAN

EVERY CREED AND CLASS.

The thought of measuring anyone's worth by the colour of their skin, or their status in life, would have been unthinkable to Newman. His vision took in a vast panorama of history in which he saw human beings who each shared the immense dignity of being called by God through their conscience. The "scum" of the Roman Empire, black slaves, ignorant peasants the poor; these formed the backbone of the early Church which passed on to future ages the image of Christ in its fullness.

It was fitting that those mixed unlettered multitudes, who for three centuries had suffered and triumphed by virtue of the inward Vision of their Divine Lord, should be selected, as we know they were, in the fourth, to be the special champions of His Divinity and the victorious foes of its impugners, at a time when the civil power, which had found them too strong for its arms, attempted, by means of a portentous heresy in the high places of the Church, to rob them of that Truth which had all along been the principle of their strength.

Grammar of Assent

STRAIGHT FROM THE HEART

PROGRESS.

As a young man, Newman rode a horse and used the stage coach. He saw the era of the train begin and revolutionize transport. He used it, and instead of looking back nostalgically at the world that had passed he turned his attention to making holy the world of the present on the principle of "nothing human is without interest to me." In one of his sermons he reveals not only his interest in the mighty powers of the steam engine but his determination not to be put off using it by the occasional accident.

You know what a sensation railway accidents occasion. Why? Because so enormous are the physical and mechanical forces which are put in motion in that mode of travelling, that, if an accident occurs, it must be gigantic. It is horrible from the conditions under which it takes place. In consequence, it impresses the imagination beyond what the reason can warrant; so that you may fall in with persons, who, on hearing, and much more, on undergoing such a misfortune, are not slow to protest that they never will travel by a railroad again. But sober men submit the matter to a more exact investigation . . . And then they contrast with the results thus obtained the corresponding results which coach travelling supplies, and they end, perhaps, by coming to the conclusion that, in matter of fact, the rail is safer than the road.
Sermons Preached on Various Occasions

THOUGHTS OF JOHN HENRY NEWMAN

A WORLD IN NEED OF COMPASSION.

Among those who preached "progress" in the late nineteenth century Newman preached compassion. For a world that history showed to be a madhouse, its inmates often weak-minded, deranged and spiritually diseased, the prophets of the new technology had really little to offer: travel by train, by car and, in the future by aeroplane. Newman would probably have been quite unsurprised by the news that the twentieth century was to see two world wars and the invention of the atomic bomb.

To consider the world in its length and breadth, its various history, the many races of man, their starts, their fortunes, their mutual alienation, their conflicts; and then their ways, habits, governments, forms of worship; their enterprises, their aimless courses, their random achievements and acquirements, the impotent conclusion of longstanding facts, the tokens so faint and broken, of a superintending design, the blind evolution of what turn out to be great powers or truths, the progress of things, as if from unreasoning elements, not towards final causes, the greatness and littleness of man, his far-reaching aims, his short duration, the curtain hung over his futurity, the disappointments of life, the defeat of good, the success of evil, physical pain, mental anguish, the prevalence and intensity of sin, the pervading idolatries, the corruptions, the dreary

STRAIGHT FROM THE HEART

hopeless irreligion, that condition of the whole race, so fearfully yet exactly described in the Apostle's words, "Having no hope and without God in the world,"—all this is a vision to dizzy and appal; and inflicts upon the mind a sense of profound mystery, which is absolutely beyond human solution.

Apologia

THOUGHTS OF JOHN HENRY NEWMAN

SOCIAL REFORM.

Newman is sometimes criticized for taking no part in the social reforms that were beginning in his day. Dickens, Mrs. Gaskell, Karl Marx, all highlighted the sub-human conditions in which so many lived. Newman felt his special call was not in the direct curing of social ills but rather in preaching the message which pinpointed the fundamental cause of them. He did, of course, work and care for the poor for most of his life, both in Oxford and Birmingham, and preached against the evils of greed for money.

The most obvious danger which worldly possessions present to our spiritual welfare is, that they become practically a substitute in our hearts for that One Object to which our supreme devotion is due . . . In this then consists the danger of the pursuit of gain . . . it is the most common and widely extended of all excitements. It is one in which everyone may indulge, nay, and will be praised by the world for indulging. And it lasts through life . . . Nor is it a slight aggravation of the evil, that anxiety is almost sure to attend it. A life of money-getting is a life of care . . . Money is a sort of creation, and gives the acquirer, even more than the possessor, an imagination of his own power; and tends to make him idolize self.

Parochial and Plain Sermons, II 28

STRAIGHT FROM THE HEART

EDUCATION.

Newman spent many years involved in teaching of one kind or another. He tutored at Oxford, was called to found the University of Ireland and established his own school in Birmingham. It is interesting to contrast his ideas on education with those of some contemporary educationalists who refer to our children as "marketable commodities" and, at times, seem to regard our schools as places for producing new and spare parts for the economic machine.

That perfection of the intellect, which is the result of education . . . to be imparted to individuals in their respective measures, is the clear, calm, accurate vision and comprehension of all things, as far as the finite mind can embrace them, each in its place, and with its own characteristics upon it. It is almost prophetic from its knowledge of history; it is almost heart-searching from its knowledge of human nature; it has almost supernatural charity from its freedom from littleness and prejudice; it has almost the repose of faith, because nothing can startle it; it has almost the beauty and harmony of heavenly contemplation, so intimate is it with the eternal order of things and the music of the spheres.

Knowledge is capable of being its own end. Such is the constitution of the human mind that any kind of knowledge, if it be really such, is its own reward.

THOUGHTS OF JOHN HENRY NEWMAN

And if this is true of all knowledge, it is true also of that special philosophy which I have made to consist in a comprehensive view of truth in all its branches ... What the worth of such an acquirement is, compared with other objects which we seek, wealth or power or honour, or the conveniences and comforts of life, I do not profess here to discuss; but I would maintain and mean to show, that it is an object in its own nature so really and undeniably good as to be the compensation of a great deal of thought in the compassing, and a great deal of trouble in the attaining.

The Idea of a University

STRAIGHT FROM THE HEART

THE FIRST SHALL BE LAST.

Victorian England seems to have had its fair share of arrogant people. Britain ruled a great empire, had led the way in industrial revolution and seemed set for a future of indefinite progress. For Newman the test of progress was the extent to which one is receptive to God's truth and faithful to His voice within. Christianity, he affirmed, was to be addressed to those whose minds were properly prepared for it. For this reason he dismissed what he called the opinions that "characterize a civilized age" and affirmed that the natural religions of many heathens were better soil for the reception of God's word.

I mean to denote those who are imbued with the religious opinions and sentiments which I have identified with Natural religion . . . it may be urged, then, that no appeal will avail me, which is made to religions so notoriously immoral as those of paganism . . . There is a better side of their teaching; purity has often been held in reverence, if not practised, ascetics have been in honour; hospitality has been a sacred duty; and dishonesty and injustice have been under a ban. Here then, as before, I take our natural perception of right and wrong as the standard for determining the characteristics of Natural Religion, and I use the religious rites and traditions which are actually found in the world . . .

Grammar of Assent

MAN OF MANY INTERESTS.

It has been said that "The glory of God is man fully alive." Known as a theologian and preacher, Newman was, in fact, a man of very varied interests and accomplishments.

THOUGHTS OF JOHN HENRY NEWMAN

POETRY.

Educated in the classics, Newman was a lover of literature. His taste in poetry embraced such names as Virgil, Homer, Shakespeare, Milton, Wordsworth, Scott; in fact, any poetry that directed the mind to what was beautiful. He was particularly fond of Wordsworth's work and the two actually met once at a breakfast party in Oxford in 1839, when Wordsworth was given an honorary degree. Wordsworth was the center of attraction, lionized by the ladies, one of whom found Newman a "poor-looking, pinched-up person," in comparison with the star of the evening. In an article written in 1858 Newman describes poetry as follows:

Poetry demands, as its primary condition, that we should not put ourselves above the objects in which it resides, but at their feet; that we should feel them to be above and beyond us . . . Poetry does not address the reason, but the imagination and affections; it leads to admiration, enthusiasm, devotion, love. The vague, the uncertain, the irregular, the sudden, are among its attributes or sources. Hence it is that a child's mind is so full of poetry, because he knows so little; and an old man of the world so devoid of poetry, because his experience of facts is so wide. Hence it is that nature is commonly more poetical than art . . . history more poetical than philosophy; the savage

STRAIGHT FROM THE HEART

than the citizen; the knight-errant than the brigadier general; the winding bridal path than the straight railroad; the sailing vessel than the steamer.

Historical Sketches

THOUGHTS OF JOHN HENRY NEWMAN

PRAISE TO THE HOLIEST.

In 1865 Newman was asked by a lady who was editing the Jesuit periodical, "The Month," if he could provide an article. He produced some scraps of paper on which he had written "The Dream of Gerontius." The poem became very popular long before Sir Edward Elgar set it to music in 1900.

Praise to the Holiest in the height,
And in the depth be praise:
In all his words most wonderful;
Most surer in all his ways.

Woe to thee, man; for he was found
A recreant in the fight;
And lost his heritage of heaven,
And fellowship with light.

Above him now the angry sky,
Around the tempest's din;
Who once had angels for his friends,
Has but the brutes for kin.

And quickened by the Almighty's breath,
And chastened by his rod,
And taught by angel visitings,
At length he sought his God.

STRAIGHT FROM THE HEART

And learned to call upon his name,
And in his faith create
A household and a fatherland,
A city and a state.

Glory to Him who from the mire,
In patient length of days,
Elaborated into life
A people to his praise.

The Dream of Gerontius

THOUGHTS OF JOHN HENRY NEWMAN

NOVELS.

Newman was a great reader of novels (he quotes Mrs. Gaskell's "North and South" in his "Grammar of Assent") and even wrote a couple himself. One, "Loss and Gain," is the story of a young man who is converted to Roman Catholicism; the other, "Callista," is a story of Christians in the third century. Agellius, a young Christian, comes to seek the hand of the maiden Callista:

Agellius took up the flowers and laid them on the table before her, as she sat at work. "Do you accept my flowers, Callista?" he asked.

"Fair and fragrant, like myself, are they?" she made reply. "Give them to me." She took them and bent over them . . . "Agellius, I once had a slave who belonged to your religion. She had been born in a Christian family, and came into my possession on her master's death. She was unlike anyone I have seen before or since; she cared for nothing yet was not morose, or peevish or hard-hearted. She died young in my service. Shortly before her end she had a dream. . . .

Callista

STRAIGHT FROM THE HEART
MUSIC.

From boyhood Newman loved music. He liked especially to play the viola in Beethoven's quartets. It was said of him that, had he put his mind to it instead of the Church, he could have been in the same class as Paganini. When he moved to Birmingham he would sometimes play the harmonium for the singing. He spoke of music as "much more than a mere sound which is gone and perishes." In "The Dream of Gerontius" the music of heaven is described.

"And hark I hear a singing; yet in sooth
I cannot of that music rightly say
Whether I hear or touch or taste the tones.
Oh what a heart-subduing melody!"

The sound is like the rushing of the wind—
The Summer wind among the lofty pines;
Swelling and dying, echoing round about,
Now here, now distant, wild and beautiful . . .

And music comes into the sermons too:

It calls in my spirits, composes my thoughts, delights my ear, recreates my mind, and so not only fits me for after business, but fills my heart, at the present, with pure and useful thoughts; so that when the

THOUGHTS OF JOHN HENRY NEWMAN

music sounds the sweetliest in my ears, truth commonly flows the clearest into my mind.

The Dream of Gerontius

STRAIGHT FROM THE HEART
ARCHTECTURE.

The style of architecture that affected Newman most powerfully seems to have been Gothic. He found it to be endowed with a "profound and commanding beauty" and regarded it as "the one true child of Christianity." He welcomed the growing attention to church architecture but was aware that there were more important things to be done. The following passage from his novel "Loss and Gain" seems to reflect his own preferences.

"I fear I must confess," said Willis, "that the churches of Rome do not affect me like the Gothic; I reverence them, I feel awe in them, but I love, I feel a sensible pleasure at the sight of the Gothic arch." "There are other reasons for that in Rome," said Campbell; "the churches are so unfinished, so untidy. Rome is a city of ruins . . . In Rome you have huge high buttresses in the place of columns and these are not cased with marble but of cold white plaster or paint. They impart an indescribable forlorn look to the churches."

Loss and Gain

THOUGHTS OF JOHN HENRY NEWMAN

THE ART OF TEACHING.

Newman was regarded in his prime as perhaps the greatest preacher in England at a time when preaching was supreme. He has been praised for his lucidity, the purity of his style and his learning. Perhaps the quality that makes him special as a teacher is his humility and his concern for his hearers, "in suggesting thoughts, which in God's good time may quietly bear fruit." Unlike the occasional self-publicist who finds the spotlight in today's media, he was most concerned for his audience. He did not wish to unsettle the mind of the unsophisticated believer. In his essay on the inspiration of Scripture, he stands for the freedom of the scholar but also for the right of the weak to their faith.

To profess the new opinion may be abstractedly permissible, but is not always permissible in practice. The novelty may be so startling as to require a full certainty that it is true; it may be so strange as to raise the question whether it will not unsettle ill-educated minds,—that is, though the statement may not be an offense against faith, still it may be an offense against charity . . . charity towards the weak and ignorant, and distrust of self, should keep a man from being impetuous or careless in circulating what nevertheless he holds to be true . . . the household of

STRAIGHT FROM THE HEART

God has claims upon our tenderness in such matters which criticism and history have not.

On the Inspiration of Scripture

THOUGHTS OF JOHN HENRY NEWMAN

CHILDREN.

Although Newman never married, he loved children and they seem to have enjoyed his company. At the height of his influence as a preacher in Oxford he surprised some earnest visitors. Instead of the famous theologian-preacher they found a young man in an armchair with two children (his friend Pusey's) on his knees. He would put his spectacles first on one and then on the other to their great delight. He then told them the story of the magic broomstick. In a sermon from 1833 he echoes something of Wordsworth's, "Our birth is but a sleep and a forgetting."

—But (the child) has this one great gift, that he seems to have lately come from God's presence, and not to understand the language of this visible scene, or how it is a temptation, how it is a veil interposing itself between the soul and God. The simplicity of a child's ways and notions, his ready belief of everything he is told, his artless love, his frank confidence, his confession of helplessness, his ignorance of evil, his inability to conceal his thoughts, his contentment, his prompt forgetfulness of trouble, his admiring without coveting; and, above all, his reverential spirit. Looking at all things about him as wonderful, as tokens and types of the One Invisible, are all evidence of his being lately (as it were) a visitant in a higher state of things. I would only have a person re-

STRAIGHT FROM THE HEART

flect on the earnestness and awe with which a child listens to any description or tale; or again, his freedom from that spirit of proud independence, which discovers itself in the soul as time goes on. And though, doubtless, children are generally of a weak and irritable nature, and all are not equally amiable, yet their passions go and are over like a shower; not interfering with the lesson we may gain to our own profit from their ready faith and guilelessness.

Parochial and Plain Sermons, II 6

THOUGHTS OF JOHN HENRY NEWMAN

COMMUNITY.

The Congregation of St. Philip Neri furnished Newman with the inspiration to do a similar work in England. No solitary, Newman like most people needed friends around him. Furthermore the community of St. Philip was in the center of a great city as a great light for the lives of those living there. Newman perceived that the England of his day was centered mainly in the great cities. For the first time in her history there were more town dwellers than country folk. He felt that his community should be where the people were. He moved with the times, exchanging the beauties of rural Oxford for the streets of Birmingham.

Those early religious lived in communities, which were detached from each other, not brought together under one common governance; they were settled in one place, and had no duties beyond it; vows were not a necessary element of their state; they had little or nothing to do with ecclesiastical matters or secular politics; they had no large plan of action for religious ends; they let each day do its work as it came; they lived in obscurity, and laid a special stress on prayer and meditation; they were simple in their forms of worship and they freely admitted laymen into their fellowship. In peculiarities such as these we recognize the Oratory of St. Philip.

Sermons Preached on Various Occasions

STRAIGHT FROM THE HEART

POLITICS.

In politics Newman showed himself to be a middle-of-the-road man. Not that he often wrote on political matters directly. When he was involved in trying to establish a Catholic university in Ireland in the early 1850s, he distanced himself from both the extreme left and right of his day in an article written to illustrate the idea of a university. It is interesting to note that, while Newman did not concern himself much with politics, one of the most vociferous Christian apologists for a more just society with a fairer distribution of wealth, Hilaire Belloc, was a pupil at Newman's oratory school for seven years.

The name of Religion is but another name for law on the one hand, freedom on the other; and at this very time, who are its professed enemies, but Socialists, Red Republicans, Anarchists and Rebels? But a Conservative, in the political sense of the word, . . . means a man who is at the top of the tree, and knows it, and means never to come down, whatever it may cost him to keep his place there. It means a man who upholds government and society and the existing state of things . . . not because it is good and desirable . . . because it is a benefit to the population, because it is full of promise for the future, but rather because he himself is well off in consequence of it, and be-

THOUGHTS OF JOHN HENRY NEWMAN

cause to take care of number one is the main political principle.

Historical Sketches

STRAIGHT FROM THE HEART

SPORT.

At school Newman did not care much for organized games. Marbles and casual cricket seem to have been the official menu! He did like swimming, however, was a great walker and rode a horse as a young man, vaulting into the saddle for exercise. While he was at Oxford, Wordsworth's nephew founded the boat race, but Newman seems hardly to have noticed. Equally unremarkable in his eyes were the founding of the football league in 1863 and the introduction of overarm bowling into cricket in 1865. In his rides and walks he enjoyed to the full the beauties of nature as this extract from a letter to his mother shows.

"What strikes me most is the strange richness of everything. The rocks blush into every variety of colour, the trees and fields are emeralds, and the cottages are rubies. A beetle I picked up ... was as green and gold as the stone it lay upon, and a squirrel which ran up a tree here just now was not the pale reddish brown to which I am accustomed, but a bright brown-red ... The exuberance of the grass and the foliage is oppressive, as if one had not room to breathe ... The scents are extremely fine, so very delicate and yet so powerful, and the colours of the flowers as if they were all shot with white. The sweet peas especially have the complexion of a beautiful face. They trail up the wall mixed with myrtles as creepers."

Letters and Correspondence, Ed. A. Mozley

STRAIGHT FROM THE HEART

ANIMALS.

Newman was fascinated by animals. From boyhood when he watched a neighbor's cockatoo through to old age when he visited zoos, he found animals strange and mysterious. He reflected on their passions and habits and speculated as to whether they are to live after this life, but concluded that "all is mystery about them." In an early work, "Church of the Fathers," he has some very solemn thoughts which arise from the life of one of the early saints who struggled against the devil.

"Certainly the sight of a beast of prey, with his malevolent passions, savage cruelty, implacable rage, malice, cunning, sullenness, restlessness, brute hunger, irresistible strength, though there cannot be sin in any of these qualities themselves, awakens very awful and complicated musings in a religious mind."

In a lighter vein he once wrote in pencil for a lady's album the following lines, "inspired" by a couple of kittens belonging to his host.

Two kittens gain our pleased caress
And share our rival praise
One has the rarer cleverness,
One beauty's winning ways.

THOUGHTS OF JOHN HENRY NEWMAN

Thoughtless of self, a friendly pair,
In musing mood they sit;
No airs deform the modest fair,
No gibe the silent wit.

Church of the Fathers
Letters and Correspondence, Ed. A. Mozley

PERSONAL GLIMPSES.

Great thinker, leader of movements, even saint; Newman has been called all these things. In these extracts we glimpse a human being who sometimes felt lonely, needed friends, was devastated by the death of dear ones, had difficult decisions to make, was often disappointed and failed in many things.

THOUGHTS OF JOHN HENRY NEWMAN

A YOUNG MAN'S THOUGHTS.

Newman wrote verse as a hobby all his life. He would have made no claim to be a poet, but his verses are always interesting, often distinguished and at times inspiring. Here is a glimpse into the mind of a young student at Oxford in 1819. He was at times rather lonely and would go for solitary walks in the countryside.

No! give me, Great Lord, the constant soul,
   Nor fooled by pleasure nor enslaved by care;
Each rebel passion (for Thou canst) control,
   And make me know the tempter's every snare
   What, though alone my sober hours I wear,
No friend in view, and sadness o'er my mind
   Throws her dark veil?—Thou but accord this prayer,
And I will bless Thee for my birth, and find
That stillness breathes sweet tones, and solitude is kind.

                        Verses on Various Occasions

STRAIGHT FROM THE HEART

LOVE THE ONE THING NEEDFUL.

Newman took great care to try and follow his own precept that love of others meant first of all loving those around us. When his father died, he looked after the family, eventually helping his mother and sisters to settle near to him at Oxford. His younger brother, Frank, he helped by tutoring him. Both brothers then took on the responsibility of Charles, their other brother who ended up living at Tenby, a socialist and atheist till the end and not too balanced either. But even while fulfilling his family duties, Newman was aware that duty was not enough and that the greatest gift of all was to be sought with prayer and sacrifice.

A smooth and easy life, an uninterrupted enjoyment of the goods of Providence, full meals, soft rainment, well-furnished homes, the pleasures of sense, the feeling of security, the consciousness of wealth,—these and the like, if we are not careful, choke up all the avenues of the soul, through which the light and breath of heaven might come to us . . . we must, at least at seasons, defraud ourselves of nature if we would not be defrauded of grace. If we attempt to force our minds into a loving and devotional temper, without this preparation, it is all too plain what will follow,—the grossness and coarseness, the affectation, the effeminacy, the unreality, the presumption,

THOUGHTS OF JOHN HENRY NEWMAN

the hollowness... in a word, what Scripture calls the Hypocrisy, which we see around us.

Parochial and Plain Sermons, V 23

STRAIGHT FROM THE HEART

DEATH OF A DEAR ONE

In Newman's diary for January 5th, 1828, we can read five words:
>*"We lost my sister Mary."*

She died suddenly on the evening of that day and her loss devastated her brother. He never recovered and to the end of his days wept at the thought of her. She was the youngest of his sisters and he was fondest of her. She was just nineteen when she died.

It was with her in mind that he preached a sermon called "Divine Calls."

Perhaps it may be the loss of some dear friend or relative through which the call comes to us; which shows us the vanity of things below and prompts us to make God our sole stay. We through grace do so in a way we never did before; and in the course of years, when we look back on our life, we find that that sad event has brought us into a new state of faith and judgment and that we are as though other men from what we were. We thought, before it took place, that we were serving God . . . but we find that . . . we were serving the world under the show and the belief of serving God.

Parochial and Plain Sermons, VIII 2

THOUGHTS OF JOHN HENRY NEWMAN

THIS IS MY LIFE.

In the early 1860s Newman was weighed down by a number of heavy crosses. His health was not good, the school he had founded was having problems, at Rome he was regarded as very suspect in his teachings. Then in 1864 he was sent a copy of a review in which Charles Kingsley had written: "Truth for its own sake has never been a virtue of the Roman clergy. Fr. Newman informs us that it need not and, on the whole, ought not to be." This roused Newman and, standing for hours at a time at the desk in his library, he traced the development of his own inner life and convictions in what became his best-known book, "Apologia Pro Vita Sua." An immediate best-seller, it was read and discussed in towns and villages throughout the land. Perhaps its most remarkable quality is its shining sincerity, illustrated in this passage where Newman recalls one of the great crises of his life which occurred in 1833 when he was on holiday in Sicily.

I began to think that I had a mission. There are sentences of my letters to my friends to this effect, if they are not destroyed. When we took leave of Monsignore Wiseman, he had courteously expressed a wish that we might make a second visit to Rome; I said with great gravity, "We have a work to do in England." I went down at once to Sicily and the presentiment grew stronger. I struck into the middle

STRAIGHT FROM THE HEART

of the island and fell ill of a fever at Leonforte. My servant thought I was dying and begged for my last directions. I gave them, as he wished; but I said, "I shall not die." I repeated, "I shall not die, for I have not sinned against light, I have not sinned against light." I never have been able to make out at all what I meant.

... Before starting from my inn in the morning on May 26th or 27th, I sat down on my bed and began to sob bitterly. My servant, who had acted as my nurse, asked what ailed me. I could only answer, "I have a work to do in England ..."

Apologia

THOUGHTS OF JOHN HENRY NEWMAN

LEAD KINDLY LIGHT.

Perhaps in this poem we have a glimpse into the very heart of Newman. He had been critically ill in Sicily at the end of his Italian holiday. "I was aching to get home; yet for want of a vessel I was kept at Palermo for three weeks ... At last I got off in an orange boat, bound for Marseilles. Then it was that I wrote the lines, 'Lead Kindly Light' which have since become well known. We were becalmed a whole week in the straits of Bonifacio." The poem is dated June 16, 1833.

   Lead, kindly Light, amid the encircling gloom,
      Lead Thou me on!
   The night is dark and I am far from home—
      Lead Thou me on!
   Keep Thou my feet; I do not ask to see
   The distant scene,—one step enough for me.

   I was not ever thus, nor prayed that Thou
      Shouldst lead me on.
   I loved to choose and see my path; but now
      Lead Thou me on!
   I loved the garish day, and, spite of fears,
   Pride ruled my will: remember not past years.

STRAIGHT FROM THE HEART

So long Thy power hath blessed me, sure it still
  Will lead me on
O'er moor and fen, o'er crag and torrent, till
  The night is gone;
And with the morn those angel faces smile
Which I have loved long since, and lost awhile.

Letters and Correspondence, Ed. A. Mozley

THOUGHTS OF JOHN HENRY NEWMAN

PEACE OF MIND.

In 1839 Newman began one of the most personally distressing periods of his life. He began to suspect that he could not in conscience stay in the Church he loved. To leave it would lose him his living, his position, his friends. He had become in the preceding years the leader of the Anglo-Catholic group in his church and was looked upon as its spokesman all over England. It was at the end of this year that he wrote his lovely sermon on "Equanimity."

... The Christian has a deep, silent, hidden peace, which the world sees not,—like some well in a retired and shady place, difficult of access. He is the greater part of his time by himself, and when he is in solitude, that is his real state. What he is when left to himself and to his God, that is his true life. He can bear himself; he can, as it were, joy in himself, for it is the grace of God within him, it is the presence of the eternal comforter in which he joys. He can bear, he finds it pleasant to be with himself at all times,— "never less alone than when alone." He can lay his head on his pillow at night, and own in God's sight, with overflowing heart, that he wants nothing.

Parochial and Plain Sermons, V 5

STRAIGHT FROM THE HEART

A FAILURE.

Newman's life was marked by failure. First at university; expected to obtain a first class degree, he just scraped a pass. Nerves beat him. Then as the virtual leader of a nationwide movement to revive the spirit of the Church in England, he felt the earth open in front of him as he tried to walk the way indicated by the light of conscience. He took his leave of his congregation with a moving request for their prayers.

O my brethren, O kind and affectionate hearts, O loving friends, should you know anyone whose lot it has been, by writing or by word of mouth, in some degree to help you thus to act; if he has ever told you what you knew about yourselves, or what you did not know; has read to you your wants or feelings, and comforted you by the very reading; has made you feel that there was a higher life than this daily one; and a brighter world than that you see; or encouraged you, or sobered you, or opened a way to the enquiring, or soothed the perplexed . . . remember such a one in time to come, though you hear him not, and pray for him, that in all things he may know God's will, and at all times he may be ready to fulfill it.

Sermons on Subjects of the Day

THOUGHTS OF JOHN HENRY NEWMAN

MORE FAILURE.

If the first part of Newman's life was marked by failure the second seemed to move from disaster to disaster. Plans to open a house at Oxford which might be a center for Catholic students came to nothing. A design for a translation of the Bible was thwarted. His attempt to found a university in Ireland proved abortive. There were problems with his community, problems with the school. He was thought for years by the authorities at Rome to be unsound in his teaching. The Catholic authorities at home for the most part did not trust him. In one humiliating episode he was arraigned in court on a charge of libel, convicted, fined and lectured by the Judge. In old age he was able to look back without bitterness and to thank God for His goodness.

Thou art careful and tender to each of the beings that Thou hast created, as if it were the only one in the whole world. For Thou canst see every one of them at once, and Thou lovest every one in this mortal life, and pursuest every one by itself, with all the fullness of thy attributes, as if Thou wast waiting on it and ministering to it for its own sake. My God I love to contemplate Thee, I love to adore Thee, thus the wonderful worker of all things every day in every place.

STRAIGHT FROM THE HEART

All Thy acts of Providence are acts of love. If Thou sendest evil upon us, it is in love. All the evils of the physical world are intended for the good of Thy creatures, or are the unavoidable attendants on that good. And Thou turnest that evil into good . . . Nothing is done in vain, but has its gracious end.

Meditations and Devotions

THOUGHTS OF JOHN HENRY NEWMAN

WHEN SHALL WE THREE MEET AGAIN?

John Henry Newman was the oldest of three brothers. Charles was one year younger, Francis four. In spite of receiving the same home influences and having the same religious background, the brothers took entirely different paths in their life and thought. Francis, after going to the East as a missionary, became a university lecturer and a humanitarian. Charles became an atheist, even trying to convert John, who was to write as the text for his brother's tombstone: "Despise not O Lord, the work of thy hands." In his "Grammar of Assent," the oldest of the brothers reflects on such differences.

Thus, of three Protestants, one becomes a Catholic, a second a Unitarian, and a third an unbeliever: How is this? The first becomes a Catholic, because he assented, as a Protestant, to the doctrine of our Lord's divinity, with a real assent and a genuine conviction . . . The second became a Unitarian, because, proceeding on the principle that Scripture was the rule of faith and that a man's private judgment was its rule of interpretation . . . he said to himself, "The word of God has been made of none effect by the traditions of men," and therefore nothing was left for him but to profess what he considered primitive Christianity, and to become a humanitarian. The third gradually subsided into infidelity because he

STRAIGHT FROM THE HEART

started with the Protestant dogma that a priesthood was the corruption of the simplicity of the Gospel ... (finally) he really did not see what scientific proof there was of the Being of God at all, and it seemed to him as if all things would go on quite as well as at present without that hypothesis ... each of the three men started with just one certitude ... He was true to that one conviction from first to last ...

Grammar of Assent

THOUGHTS OF JOHN HENRY NEWMAN

DEAR MR. GLADSTONE.

When in 1870 the Pope was declared infallible by the Roman Catholic Church, Mr. Gladstone, in company with many others, including some Catholics, understood this to mean that the Pope was inspired by God whenever he spoke and that Catholics would be bound to obey him, even if he were to command them, for instance, to overthrow Queen Victoria. Such ideas may seem overwhelmingly silly today but Gladstone put them into a best-selling pamphlet to which Newman was pursuaded to reply. Protocol dictated that the answer should be in the form of a letter to the Duke of Norfolk in which Newman simply pointed out that infallibility is rather like a brake to prevent the Church from running into error, not a constant whisper from on high ordering people what to do in every detail of their lives.

I own to a deep feeling that Catholics may in good measure thank themselves, and no one else, for having alienated from them so religious a mind (as Mr. Gladstone). A feeling was too prevalent in many places that no one could be true to God and His Church who had any pity on troubled souls ... it was the fashion to call writers who conformed to this rule of the Church (to add nothing to the Church's teaching) by the name of minimizers ... To be a true Cath-

STRAIGHT FROM THE HEART

olic a man must have a generous loyalty towards ecclesiastical authority but . . . has a claim to be met and handled with a wise and gentle minimism.

Difficulties Felt by Anglicans

THOUGHTS OF JOHN HENRY NEWMAN

LIFE'S PURPOSE.

In his last years Newman attained great tranquillity and wisdom as he continued to meditate on the ways of God in the light of his own long life's experience.

God has created me to do Him some definite service; He has committed some work to me which He has not committed to another. I have my mission—I never may know it in this life, but I shall be told it in the next. Somehow I am necessary for His purposes, as necessary in my place as an archangel in his—if, indeed, I fail, He can raise another, as He could make the stones children of Abraham. Yet I have a part in this great work; I am a link in a chain, a bond of connection between persons. He has not created me for naught. I shall do good, I shall do His work; I shall be an angel of peace, a preacher of truth in my own place, while not intending it, if I do but keep His commandments and serve Him in my calling.

Therefore I will trust Him.

Meditations and Devotions

STRAIGHT FROM THE HEART

THE END.

When Newman approached the end to enter the deepest darkness of all, he had already expressed his hopes in the epitaph he wrote, "Ex umbris et imaginibus in veritatem," "From mists and shadows into the real world." It is on his grave at Rednal today where he is buried next to his friend, Ambrose St. John. In "The Dream of Gerontius" he had pictured the Christian approaching the throne of God in the company of a guardian angel.

Softly and gently, dearest, sweetest soul,
In my most loving arms I now enfold thee,
And, o'er the penal waters, as they roll,
I poise thee, and I lower, and I hold thee.

And carefully I dip thee in the lake,
And thou, without a sob or a resistance,
Dost through the flood thy rapid passage take,
Sinking deep, deeper into the dim distance.

Angels to whom the willing task is given,
Shall tend, and nurse, and lull thee, as thou liest,
And Masses on the earth, and prayers in heaven,
Shall aid thee at the throne of the most highest.

THOUGHTS OF JOHN HENRY NEWMAN

Farewell, but not for ever! brother dear,
Be brave and patient on thy bed of sorrow;
Swiftly shall pass thy night of trial here,
And I will come and wake thee on the morrow.

Dream of Gerontius

SUGGESTED FURTHER READINGS.

THERE is a vast literature associated with Newman, much of it concerned with various aspects of his theology. The reader who is new to his writing will find in the source list at the end of this selection some titles of Newman's own writings. Perhaps the easiest to obtain is the *Apologia Pro Vita Sua* which has gone through many editions and can be obtained in paperback or hardback without difficulty. It may well prove the best opening for anyone who wishes to delve further into Newman's writings. For those interested in education, Newman's *Idea of a University* has been reprinted often and is available in an Image paperback from Doubleday. For anyone of a philosophical bent Newman's lifelong concern with the relationship between reason and belief can best be explored in his *University Sermons*, an SPCK paperback, and his *Grammar of Assent*, available in an Image paperback from Doubleday. His two novels *Loss and Gain* and *Callista* were put out in paperback by Universe books and may still be obtainable. *Medi-*

tations and Devotions has been reprinted many times, and second hand copies can be found.

The Friends of Cardinal Newman, based at the Birmingham Oratory, have a selection of his works both new and second hand and supply a list on request.

For those anxious to know more about the life of Newman Ian Ker's *John Henry Newman* (Oxford Univ. Press) is the latest and, perhaps, the best biography. It is, however, costly and a more practical buy for most people must be Meriol Trevor's paperback, *Newman's Journey* (Fontana), an abridgement of her two-volume work of 1962.

Newman's thought has attracted scholars worldwide to comment on and develop it. Perhaps the best introduction is *John Henry Newman* by Fr. C.S. Dessain, who was an outstanding Newman scholar and a member of the Birmingham Oratory. Short, well written and scholarly, it is available in an Oxford Univ. Press paperback.

BIBLIOGRAPHY

Main Works of J.H. Newman Used in this Anthology

The Arians of the Fourth Century, 1833.
Parochial and Plain Sermons (8 Vols), 1834-43.
Church of the Fathers, 1840.
Sermons on Subjects of the Day, 1843.
University Sermons, 1843.
Loss and Gain, 1848.
Callista, 1855.
Historical Sketches, 1856.
Sermons Preached on Various Occasions, 1857.
Idea of a University, 1859.
Apologia Pro Vita Sua, 1864.
The Dream of Gerontius, 1865.
Verses on Various Occasions, 1867.
An Essay in Aid of a Grammar of Assent, 1870.
Difficulties Felt by Anglicans, 1875.
On the Inspiration of Scripture, 1884.
Letters and Correspondence of J.H.N.,
   ed. A. Mozley, 1890.
Meditations and Devotions, 1893.